Emmitt Smith

by Mark Stewart

PHOTO CREDITS

All photos courtesy AP/Wide World Photos, Inc. except the following:

Vincent Manniello/Sports Chrome – 6, 9
Rich Kane/Sports Chrome – Cover
Robert Tringali, Jr./Sports Chrome – 13, 28, 35, 43
Sports Chrome – 5 center right
Tom DiPace – 4 center right, 4 bottom right, 16, 17, 24 top, 29, 42
Mark Stewart – 48

STAFF

Project Coordinator: John Sammis, Cronopio Publishing
Series Design Concept: The Sloan Group
Design and Electronic Page Makeup: Jaffe Enterprises, and
        Digital Communications Services, Inc.

LIBRARY OF CONGRESS CATALOGING-IN-PUBLICATION DATA

Stewart, Mark.
    Emmitt Smith / by Mark Stewart.
        p. cm. – (Grolier All-Pro Biographies biographies)
    Includes index.
    Summary: A brief biography of the star running back who helped the Dallas Cowboys win
Super Bowls in 1993, 1994, and 1996.
    ISBN 0-516-20169-7 (lib. binding)-ISBN 0-516-26017-0 (pbk.)
    1. Smith, Emmitt, 1969-   –Juvenile literature. 2. Football players–United States–Biography–
Juvenile literature. 3. Dallas Cowboys (Football team)–Juvenile literature. [1. Smith, Emmitt,
1969-   . 2. Football players. 3. Afro-Americans–Biography.] I. Title. II. Series.
GV939.S635S84 1996
796.332'092–dc20
[B]   96-20084
                                                                                        CIP
                                                                                        AC

Grolier ALL-PRO Biographies™

Emmitt Smith

by
Mark Stewart

CHILDREN'S PRESS®
A Division of Grolier Publishing
New York • London • Hong Kong • Sydney
Danbury, Connecticut

Contents

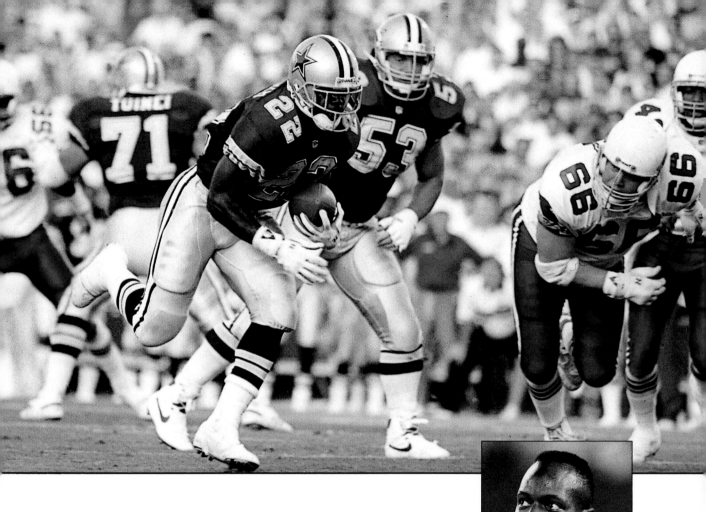

Emmitt Smith

He sees things other athletes do not. He can predict the outcome of plays before they even begin. And it has been that way for him from the first time he touched a football. He is already one of the best football players in history, but in his mind the best is yet to come. His name is Emmitt Smith, and this is his story . . .

Growing Up

To succeed in the National Football League, you need strength, coordination, desire, and a love of football. According to Emmitt Smith's mother, her son possessed these qualities before his first birthday. Emmitt would climb up his crib railing, lower himself to the floor, and crawl into the living room, where his mother and father were watching football on TV. Then little Emmitt would rock himself to sleep.

The Smiths, who lived in Pensacola, Florida, were a football family. Emmitt's uncles and cousins loved football, and he joined in their games as soon as he was old enough. Emmitt's father, a bus driver, also played safety for the Pensacola Wings of the semipro Dixie League. By the time Emmitt was five years old, everyone recognized that he had a natural talent for the game. He could perform any move he was told to try. When he joined the local Mini-Mite League at age eight, he was like nothing anyone had ever seen. "I was a step ahead of the other kids, as

Emmitt has shown great athletic ability all his life.

Dallas Cowboys quarterback Roger Staubach was Emmitt's childhood hero.

far as running the football," says Emmitt. "I was scoring touchdowns and outrunning people all the time, and it was that way all through community league football. I was almost unstoppable."

Emmitt started his career as quarterback. His hero was Roger Staubach of the Dallas Cowboys, so he asked for a jersey with Staubach's number 12. In Emmitt's second season of organized ball, his coach switched him to running back. Starting a few steps behind the line of scrimmage, Emmitt was able to scan the defense and see where the holes would be. At first, he assumed every runner could see these things. Later, he learned that this was a very special gift.

By age 10, Emmitt had been promoted to the Midget level, where he was competing against older boys. He played linebacker and ran back kicks, but he was only a second-string runner. Still, Emmitt had a lot of fun because he got to do a little of everything. The following season, Emmitt had grown so large that he was constantly in danger of weighing more than the league maximum. In order to make sure he made his weight, the team's coach, Charlie Edgar, had his star runner sleep at his house the night before games. He did not want to lose his biggest weapon to a triple cheeseburger and fries! "Coach Edgar didn't starve me," smiles Emmitt, "but he fed me low-fat foods. Then, on Saturday morning, I'd wake up and run off those last few pounds. Looking back on it, those Friday nights were important. The Edgar family was white, and even though I'd competed against some white kids, I'd never slept in a white person's home. It was a great education—a positive one. Watching the Edgars, I saw that white families were close-knit, too. I realized the Edgars were beautiful people, who embraced me like one of their own."

Emmitt's parents were proud of his success on the field, but they wanted to make sure he worked just as hard in the classroom. He was not allowed to play after school until his homework was done, and there was no way the Smiths would tolerate poor grades. Emmitt was a bright student who did his work and minded his teachers. His favorite class was math, right through junior high and high school. "I loved the numbers and the fractions and the geometric theorems," he says.

By the time Emmitt enrolled at Escambia High School, he was the best young athlete in town. He was everyone's favorite, on and off the field, and he always seemed to be the center of attention. Yet Emmitt was polite and modest, despite the fact that he singlehandedly turned the school's football program around. Indeed, coach Dwight Thomas admits he had only three plays: hand-off to Emmitt, pitch-out to Emmitt, and throw to Emmitt!

A look at Emmitt's stats reveals that all three plays must have worked well. He ran for 115 yards in his very first game and led Escambia to its first winning season in seven years. As a sophomore, Emmitt scored 26 touchdowns, rushed for 2,424 yards, and helped Escambia win the Florida Division 3-A championship. Despite a variety of defenses designed specifically to stop him, Emmitt just got better and better. During his junior year, he ran for 2,918 yards and led Escambia to a 13–0 record and the state title. Emmitt's stats would have been even better that year had he played more than two or three quarters a game. But Escambia almost always had a huge lead by halftime, so Coach Thomas often sent in the second unit to finish off games. As a senior, in fact, Emmitt gained less than 2,000 yards. Still, he finished with a state record 8,804 career yards and was recognized as one of the top prep runners in the United States. Emmitt was courted by more than 200 colleges, and he was selected to represent the nation's high-school athletes at the White House ceremony when President Ronald Reagan unveiled his "Just Say No" antidrug campaign. Emmitt stepped up to the microphone and made his parents proud. "I tried to learn the right things from my mother and father," he told the crowd. "They were my heroes."

Among the many honors bestowed upon Emmitt in his senior year was *Parade* magazine's High School Player of the Year award. He and a friend were flown to California to watch the Super Bowl. While sitting in the stands at the Rose Bowl watching the Giants and Broncos locked in combat, Emmitt predicted that he would be playing in the Super Bowl himself one day. But first, he would continue his education.

Emmitt Smith always dreamed of being a successful running back in the NFL.

College

Emmitt Smith had his choice of colleges. With a B average and a string of broken records to his credit, he was looked upon as the ideal student-athlete. Football powerhouses Auburn and Nebraska made tempting offers to Emmitt, but he decided to stay close to his home in Pensacola and attend the University of Florida. He liked the fact that Florida featured a high-powered running attack, and he thought it was a sign of good luck that the team was called the Gators, just like Escambia High.

Florida coach Galen Hall liked what he saw of his freshman runner in fall practice, but decided to work him into the starting lineup slowly. When Emmitt complained, Coach Hall tried to explain that there was a big difference between darting and weaving through high-school defenses and doing the same thing against bigger, faster, smarter college players. The Gators lost their first game 31–4 as Emmitt ran the ball just five times. The following week, he was on the bench again. When Emmitt

Years

finally got into the game, he took a hand-off and scampered 66 yards for a touchdown, and carried nine more times for an additional 43 yards. That was enough to convince Coach Hall to bench his starting running back and give the freshman a chance.

Emmitt made the most of that chance. In his first game as a starter—in front of a national television audience—he smashed the school record with 224 yards on 39 carries as he chewed up the University of Alabama defense in a thrilling 23–14 victory. "All the hype had been on Alabama running back Bobby Humphrey," recalls Emmitt. "No one knew about me. I figured this was my opportunity to shine, especially as my parents were there."

Emmitt kept on rolling, finishing the season with 1,341 yards and 13 touchdowns to earn Freshman of the Year honors and become the first Florida freshman ever to be named to the All-SEC team. He finished a disappointing ninth in the Heisman

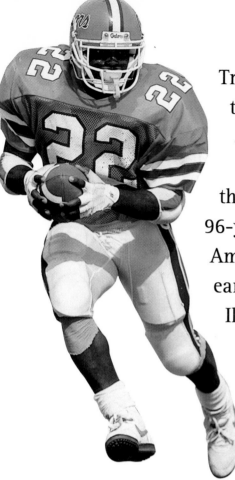

As a sophomore, Emmitt led the Gators to the All-American Bowl.

Trophy voting, an injustice that moved one teammate to say he was tempted to steal the award and give it to Emmitt!

Emmitt continued to break records for the Gators. As a sophomore, he ran for a 96-yard touchdown and led the team to the All-American Bowl, where he gained 159 yards and earned MVP honors in a 14–10 win over Illinois. One day, after scoring a touchdown, he did a little dance in the end zone. When he returned to his house in Pensacola, he expected hugs and congratulations from his parents. Instead, he got grim stares. "We'll have no more of that dancing," ordered his father. Emmitt was a national sensation—except in his own home! Needless to say, it was the last time anyone ever saw him celebrate in the end zone.

Everyone was expecting Emmitt to have a super season as a junior, but instead it was a disaster. Coach Hall resigned in October and then quarterback Kyle Morris was suspended for gambling. For the rest of the season, opponents focused on Emmitt, and he took a merciless pounding. The Gators managed

A 1988 injury kept Emmitt from compiling an incredible three straight 1,000-yard seasons in college:

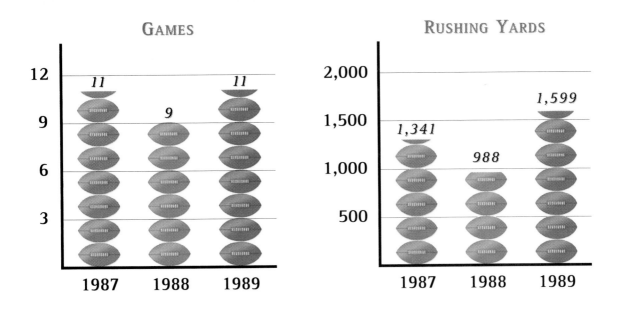

GAMES

1987	1988	1989
11	9	11

RUSHING YARDS

1987	1988	1989
1,341	988	1,599

to win seven games and earn a spot in the Freedom Bowl, but there they were overwhelmed by Washington. Emmitt had the worst day of his life, gaining just 17 yards. It did not make him feel any

better that he was recognized as an All-American. He was a team player, and the team had not been successful. Emmitt felt that things would get even worse in 1990, so he opted to skip his senior year and enter the NFL draft.

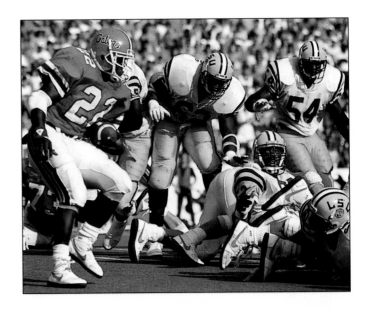

Road to the

Emmitt Smith was a certain first-round pick in the 1990 NFL draft, but it was difficult to predict just when he would be selected. Some said he was too short, some claimed he was prone to injury, and he did not have the raw speed of other top backs. Little did Emmitt know that his biggest fan worked for his favorite team. Joe Brodsky, the backfield coach of the Dallas Cowboys, had watched Emmitt's career with great interest. The Cowboys had drafted receiver Michael Irvin in 1988 and quarterback Troy Aikman in 1989. Now they needed a tough, durable runner to complete the picture. Brodsky, who had been a running back for Florida, saw Emmitt as that player. The Cowboys, however, were not sure they could get Emmitt. Dallas had the 21st pick and feared Emmitt would be taken between 16 and 20. So the team "traded up" and grabbed Emmitt with the 17th selection in the first round.

Super Bowl

Emmitt was glad to be a Cowboy, but he knew this was not the same team he had followed as a kid. In the two seasons before he arrived, Dallas had won just four games. The Super Bowl certainly looked a long way off. Still, there were encouraging signs. When the Cowboys let Emmitt run the ball, it took much of the pressure off Aikman, who was then able to connect with his receivers. The team finished 7–9 and Emmitt was named NFL Offensive Rookie of the Year.

In 1991, Emmitt fulfilled all expectations by leading the league in rushing and becoming the youngest player in history to top 1,500 yards.

In his rookie year, Emmitt helped the Cowboys win four more games than they had the year before.

More important, Dallas made the playoffs for the first time since 1985. The Irvin-Aikman-Smith trio was beginning to flex its muscles. Perhaps, thought Emmitt, the Super Bowl was not so far away after all.

By the end of Emmitt's second year, the trio of Aikman (left), Smith, and Irvin (right) had become a force in the NFL.

Emmitt nails down the 1992 rushing title with this run that resulted in a touchdown.

To the great delight of Emmitt and his teammates, everything came together in 1992, as the Cowboys went 13–3. Emmitt rushed for 1,713 yards and scored 19 touchdowns to earn All-Pro honors for the first time. In the playoffs, he scored a touchdown as Dallas whipped the Philadelphia Eagles. Then he scored two more to lead the Cowboys over the San Francisco 49ers in the NFC Championship Game. Emmitt had made it to the Super Bowl just six years after he sat in the stands as a spectator. And what a day he had, running for 108 yards and a touchdown as the Cowboys demolished the Buffalo Bills 52–17.

The remarkable rise of the Cowboys had football fans around the country arguing who was the team's most valuable player. Aikman had won the MVP award in the Super Bowl, and he deserved it, but many felt that the addition of Emmitt had made Dallas a championship franchise. Emmitt did not care to get involved in this debate. All he cared about was that the team was the best. As far as he was concerned, everyone was equally valuable.

Unfortunately, the Cowboys disagreed. During the summer of 1993, the team refused to pay Emmitt as much as it paid Aikman. So Emmitt refused to play. It took humbling losses in the season's first two games for the Cowboys to see the light, and they quickly signed their star runner to a contract that made him the highest-paid back in history. Emmitt rewarded the Cowboys with an incredible year. He topped the league in rushing despite missing the first two games, and led a furious Dallas charge back to the division title. No one was surprised when he was named Player of the Year.

The Cowboys cruised through the playoffs and

Emmitt fights Buffalo's Darryl Talley for yards during the 1993 Super Bowl.

1994 Super Bowl MVP Emmitt Smith

reached the Super Bowl again. In a return match with the Bills, Emmitt shook off the ill effects of a separated shoulder and barreled through the Buffalo defense for 132 yards. His two second-half touchdowns broke open a tie game and gave Dallas a lead they would never relinquish. At game's end, he was named Super Bowl MVP. As always, Emmitt credited his teammates with enabling him to have a big game. "The offensive line did a great job," he says. "They opened up holes for me to run the football. They controlled the whole line of scrimmage in the second half."

Emmitt led the NFL with 21 rushing touchdowns in 1994, but for the first time in four years he was not the league's top ground gainer. In 1995, however, he was back at the top of the list, with 1,773 yards and all-time best 25 rushing touchdowns. Of course, what mattered most to Emmitt was that the Cowboys made it back to the Super Bowl, where they beat the Pittsburgh Steelers 27–17. That he scored the game-clincher with 3:43 to go was just icing on the cake.

Timeline

1989:
Becomes
first Florida
running back
ever to earn
All-American
honors

**1992: Leads NFL
with 18 rushing
touchdowns**

1990:
Drafted
by Dallas
Cowboys

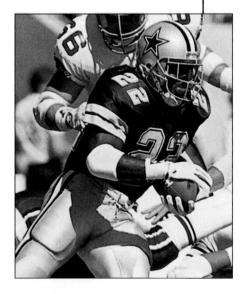

1993: Named NFL Player of the Year

1996: Scores clinching touchdown in Super Bowl XXX

1994: Honored as MVP of Super Bowl XXVIII

**Walter Payton of the
Chicago Bears**

Game

Emmitt plans to keep playing until he surpasses Walter Payton's mark of 16,726 rushing yards. "I want to get to the top, and the ultimate top is Payton's record."

The Cowboys would do anything for Emmitt because they know he would do anything for them.

I want to be known as a total team player. I play the game for my teammates first and then for myself."

Action!

Emmitt's blocking skills are often overlooked. Many feel that, pound-for-pound, he is one of the most skilled blockers in the league.

Emmitt picks up most of his yards running inside, where defenders can hit him from all sides. Remarkably, he rarely fumbles the football.

Emmitt ignored all of the pre-draft criticism in 1990. He knew he was a potential NFL All-Pro, even if his size and speed did not measure up to other backs in the draft. "They can't measure the size of a player's heart . . . and that's what they left out of my scouting report."

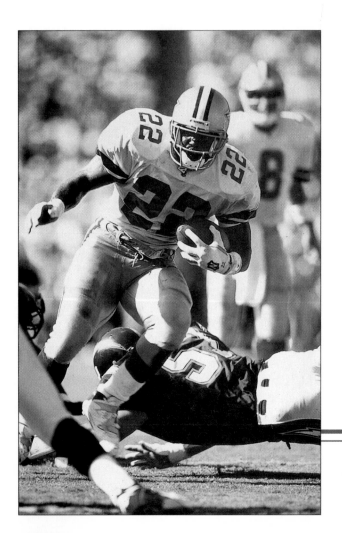

Emmitt seems to know where his blockers will go in any situation.

Emmitt's running strategy starts even before the play begins. "I stand back there before the snap and visualize my linemen making their blocks and it's like I know where the problems are before they come up."

Emmitt "freezes" tacklers by shuffling his feet and then explodes away from them at sharp angles. His balance and acceleration are incredible.

Emmitt believes he can be the best runner in history. He feels that the secret to maintaining his current level of performance is to not be satisfied with what he has already accomplished.

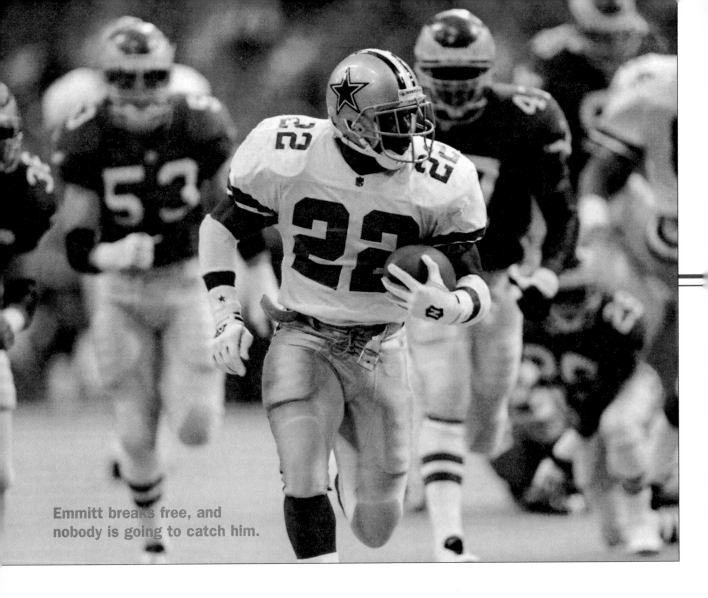

Emmitt breaks free, and
nobody is going to catch him.

Emmitt is proud to be recognized as one of the greatest players in Dallas Cowboys history, and he hopes to have his name included in Dallas's "Ring of Honor"—its Hall of Fame. "But that's a long way down the road," says Emmitt. "Right now, I just want to go and chomp up as much yardage as I can."

Emmitt may not break any records when he is running against a stopwatch. But when he breaks free in the open field, he is almost impossible to catch from behind. "Rushing with a football is like being chased by a dog–the thought of someone trying to get you makes you keep going!"

Emmitt gobbles up yards against the Green Bay Packers.

Dealing

In the final game of the 1993 season, the Cowboys needed a win over the New York Giants to win the division and get home-field advantage for the playoffs. Midway through the contest, Emmitt separated his shoulder. Realizing his team did not stand a chance without him, he stayed in the game. Each time he was tackled, the pain was practically unbearable, but he inspired his team to a 16–13 overtime victory with 168 yards on 32 carries.

"I never felt pain like that before. Every time I got knocked down, it hurt. My high-school coach, Dwight Thomas, called me from Pensacola. Dwight said he'd watched the Giants game on TV and had never seen a more courageous performance. The pain he knew I was in had brought tears to his eyes, he said. I choked up myself when Dwight said that. All these years and my coach was still proud of me!"

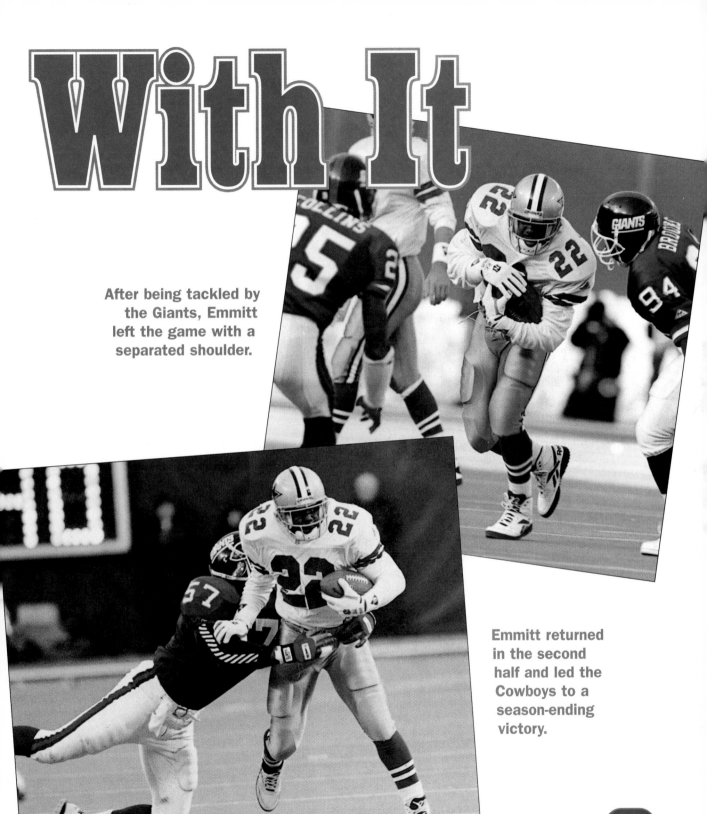

With It

After being tackled by the Giants, Emmitt left the game with a separated shoulder.

Emmitt returned in the second half and led the Cowboys to a season-ending victory.

How Does

When Emmitt spots a hole, he can cut to it immediately.

He Do It?

Emmitt Smith may be the best running back ever when it comes to spotting openings and bursting through them. His great peripheral vision—and his ability to read the defense—actually enable him to anticipate where those openings will occur. In high school, Emmitt would sometimes close his eyes and run toward a spot he thought would open for him—even when it was jammed up before the ball was snapped!

"It's not a blur, but a real clear picture. I can see things others can't see, I can see holes in coverage. Sometimes I can even predict where the hole will be."

The Grind

Most athletes who leave college early never return. Although Emmitt Smith skipped his senior year at the University of Florida to start his professional career, he understood the importance of completing his education. The life of an NFL superstar, however, can be very hectic, and it was difficult for Emmitt to find time to continue his studies. It would have been easy to wait until his playing career was over, but he had promised his mother that he would go back and finish what he started. So Emmitt simply made time. He went to class and completed his degree in public recreation. Six years after entering the NFL, Emmitt graduated from Florida as a member of the Class of '96. He received a thunderous ovation from his fellow students as he accepted his diploma.

"I'm just as thrilled about this accomplishment as I am about any other accomplishment I have achieved over the past six years. . . . It's one thing to be accepted for your athletic ability. It's another thing to be standing in an academic arena, to walk across the stage, and to be recognized for your academic accomplishment. It was special to hear that cheer."

Emmitt acknowledges the crowd's applause as he goes to accept his diploma.

Say What?

What are football people saying about Emmitt Smith?

"When you think Emmitt has reached his peak, all of a sudden he goes off and does something a little better."

—Nate Newton, Cowboys teammate

"He can put a team on his back and carry it."

—Darryl Talley, All-Pro linebacker

"I think what sets Emmitt apart from most running backs is his strength, his ability to break tackles, his balance, his blocking, and his vision"

—Joe Brodsky, Cowboys running back coach

"What I admire most about him is that he knows that he has to perform week in and week out for the team to be successful, and he shows up every week and produces."

—*Tony Dorsett, Dallas Cowboys legend*

"He's almost impossible to stop, especially in the open field."

—*Eric Allen, New Orleans Saints cornerback*

"You cannot practice defending against the way he runs."

—*Bill Curry, former NFL great*

"After watching and playing against them all, I think he's the best."

—*Tony Dungy, Tampa Bay Buccaneers head coach*

Career

Emmitt has earned NFL All-Pro honors four times in his career.

Emmitt fights for yardage during the 1996 Pro Bowl.

Emmitt earned All-America recognition in all three of his years at the University of Florida. He was a first-team pick in 1989. He was voted All-SEC in each of his three college seasons.

Emmitt averaged a league-leading 5.3 yards per carry in 1993, and was named NFL Player of the Year.

Highlights

In 1993, Emmitt became the only runner in history to miss two games and still win the rushing title.

Emmitt Smith's goal is to retire as the NFL's all-time leading rusher. He stands an excellent chance of reaching that goal. Emmitt is talented, durable, and has a great group of players blocking for him. If he retired tomorrow, however, he would already own or share a number of impressive records. Emmitt is the only player ever to notch five consecutive seasons with more than 1,400 rushing yards, while his 25 touchdowns in 1995 established a new NFL single-season mark.

Emmitt scores during the 1996 Super Bowl.

Emmitt scored his 100th NFL touchdown in his 93rd game. No one has reached the century mark faster.

Emmitt has been selected to play in the Pro Bowl every year of his career.

Emmitt's 11 100-yard rushing games in 1995 broke the old team record of nine, which was set by Tony Dorsett in 1981.

When Emmitt scored the game-clinching touchdown against the Steelers in Super Bowl XXX, it tied him with Thurman Thomas for the most post-season touchdowns, with 18. His six 100-yard rushing games in the playoffs tie him with Thomas and John Riggins.

Emmitt celebrates his record-setting 1996 Super Bowl touchdown.

Barring injury, Emmitt should break the all-time record for rushing touchdowns during the 1996 season. Walter Payton, with 110, has held the record since 1987.

Reaching

Emmitt always has time for young fans.

Out

Offensive linemen Kevin Gogan (left) and Erik Williams are two linemen who have been on the receiving end of Emmitt's generosity.

After every football season, Emmitt Smith reaches out to the guys who make his 1,000-yard seasons possible: the Dallas Cowboys offensive linemen. Emmitt started this tradition in 1991, after leading the NFL in rushing for the first time. He gave beautiful, expensive watches to Nate Newton, Mark Tuinei, Mark Stepnoski, Kevin Gogan, and Erik Williams. In 1992, he commissioned sports artist Vernon Wells to paint portraits of eight Dallas linemen and blocking back Moose Johnston. In 1993, Emmitt presented his "hole-punchers" with round-trip plane tickets to anywhere they wanted to go! The tradition has continued each February.

Numbers

Name: Emmitt Smith III

Born: May 15, 1969

Height: 5' 9"

Weight: 210 pounds

Uniform Number: 22

College: University of Florida

Emmitt is one of only four players to lead the NFL in rushing three straight years. The others are Hall-of-Famers Jim Brown, Earl Campbell, and Steve Van Buren.

Year	Team	Att	Yds	Avg	TD	Rec	Yds	Avg	TD
1990	Dallas Cowboys	241	937	3.9	11	24	228	9.5	0
1991	Dallas Cowboys	365*	1,563*	4.3	12	49	258	5.3	1
1992	Dallas Cowboys	373	1,713*	4.6	18*	59	335	5.7	1
1993	Dallas Cowboys	283	1,486*	5.3*	9	57	414	7.3	1
1994	Dallas Cowboys	368*	1,484	4.0	21*	50	341	6.8	1
1995	Dallas Cowboys	377*	1,773*	4.7	25*	62	375	6.0	0
Totals		2,007	8,956	4.5	96	301	1,951	6.5	4

*Led League

Glossary

COMMISSIONED appointed or assigned a professional to perform a service

CONSECUTIVE several events that follow one after the other

DURABLE long-lasting in spite of much use and wear

HYPE publicity; extra attention

MODEST free from conceit or vanity

PERIPHERAL VISION having an extended field of vision; the ability to see things from many angles

POTENTIAL the ability to grow and change

PRONE likely to; having a tendency toward

RELINQUISH to give up possession or power

SCALE to climb

THEOREM a mathematical formula believed to be true

Index

About The Author

Mark Stewart grew up in New York City in the 1960s and 1970s—when the Mets, Jets, and Knicks all had championship teams. As a child, Mark read everything about sports he could lay his hands on. Today, he is one of the busiest sportswriters around. Since 1990, he has written close to 500 sports stories for kids, including profiles on more than 200 athletes, past and present. A graduate of Duke University, Mark served as senior editor of *Racquet*, a national tennis magazine, and was managing editor of *Super News*, a sporting goods industry newspaper. He is the author of every Grolier All-Pro Biography.